Footfalls

By Michael FitzGerald

Cover photo graciously provided by
Nancy and Guy Cantwell

For Cyndy ...who thought I should do it...

For Harmon Arroyo ...who helped me do it...

For my family and friends ...who made it
worth doing...

MF

Footfalls

I. the way the rain falls...

The Way the Rain Falls	10
The Cabin	11
Through the Rainbow	12
Memory Rain	12
Cloud Cycle	13
Continental Divide	14
Late Sun	15
River Canyon	16
If I Was An Alien	17
In the Meantime	18
On Reading Rexroth's Japanese Poems	19
Nothing	20
The Bridge	20
Spring Forward, Fall Back	21
Spring Sun	21
The Illahee	22

II. head home together...

Runaway	24
Water Bearer	25
Rainy Day in the Little Woods	26
Night Rain	27

Uta 1   28
Uta 2   28
In a Dark Dawn   29
Weekend in Victoria   30
Just North of Clifden   31
Drawing From Memory   32
The Trail of Your Life   33
Merry-Go-Round   34

III. impatience ...

Impatience   36
A Far Morning   37
In Wonderland   38
Looking Over My Shoulder   39
Tanning   40
Spinning in the Dizzy Dance   41
The Big Bang   42

IV. holding on...

Holding On   44
For Craig   45
Gibberish   46
Morning Tea Jitters   47
Intensive Care   48
The Last Testament   49
Night Terrors   50
Pre-Dawn   51

V. a river that flows...

There is a River   54
Friends Long Absent   55
Hōw I Like It   56
She Comes To Me   57
Scales   58
Rain   59
Whatever Came Next   60
The Weight   61
Baby Girl   62
Repairs   63
Gone Again   63
Wishes   64
One Day   64
Paradelle at 50   65
Wedding Poem   66
Grandpa's Teeth   67
Years in the Grave   68
Zechariah and Gabriel   69
Father and Son   70
Father Turns Seventy   71
Who Knows What A Father Thinks?   72
Words Not Spoken   73
The Face in the Mirror   74
Dream Father   75

VI. cannot unlearn the heart...

Love in a Red Field   78
First Mountains   79
Lover of God   80
Game Day Street Preacher   81
Mornings Deep in Winter   82
Sent From God   83
The Revised Standard Version   84
The Tribal Flute Player   85
Star Sonnet   86
Sky Tree   87
Love in a Blue Sky   88

Afterword   89

I. the way the rain falls...

The Way the Rain Falls

The way the rain falls
filling the gray morning…
The way the river runs
in a storm…
The way fog swirls into the bay at dusk
over darkening waters…
The way thoughts drift out of mind
into the cold world…
The way sleep comes slowly
and the day becomes something else…

All these ways are one way -
the way of the world as it breathes.

The Cabin

A pathway,
overgrown and fragrant,
winds past memories
of rain and sun.

The end seems not far,
but paved steps are few
and run in circles.

Home is a gray mist
embracing a simple structure -
roof, walls, door, window.

The garden keeps company
with the wild
while the wind breathes slowly.

No path leads home
until the traveler
makes the journey.

Time is a weathered gift...
untamed, relentless, free.

Through the Rainbow

A curtain of rain drops
across a highway headed west,
while the setting sun colors
a rainbow on the fabric.

Driving through the rainbow,
my car keeps none of the color
and I keep none of the hope,
as I continue into the darkening east.

Memory Rain

All through the long years,
I remember rain falling
across the line of my vision,
as my eyes sought what they
did not know.

Somewhere, somehow over the years
that rain came inside and found
a place within me, where
it has lived happily since -
a joyous rain that touches me
when the dry world is too dreary.

Cloud Cycle

I
The sun springs through
a clearing in the clouds,
begging forgiveness for the night.
It rainbows to earth
crying, crying for life.

II
Standing in the still heat,
silent formations of clouds
keep a dutiful watch,
sentinels at the outposts
of two kingdoms.

III
Hot ashen clouds
cast in repentance,
weeping trees seeking benedictions,
grieve the passing graces and
lost mercies of summer.

IV
The moon lies low in the western sky,
gilting the edges of morning clouds
that shroud the island winter...
Anchored in the frozen dark,
they drift slowly at dawn.

Continental Divide

Rock cuts through a mountain,
opening to a high plain
just this side of spring.
Trees point to the invisible
as their shadows shy away.

Clouds make their way east,
trailing themselves as they go.
The sun wakes late,
warming its way slowly west.

A solitary perching bird watches
and waits for life to make a move.

Late Sun

Late sun seen through the cloudy canyon
casts odd, occasional shadows
over patches of mountain snow.
Air is scarce and breathing hard.

Far below, the Colorado runs
in and out of ice
on its way to the desert.

Winding slowly along the track,
the train is halting, hesitant, uneasy
as if anticipating ambush.

Against all logic comes a desire
to leave a fingerprint
in a passing snowbank -
a life soon gone passed through here.

River Canyon

Above the river canyon in the sunset,
a solitary bird is on the wing...
circling,
circling,
circling,
it searches for something shadowed below.

The wind echoes itself endlessly,
creating an illusion of emptiness
in the dark chasm of the deep.
Tinged with the light of a dying day,
the soaring one watches and waits.

If I Was An Alien

If I was an alien,
I might think the blowing
leaves are alive.

I might marvel at how still
they lie for long periods of time -
and how quickly they begin
their dance with the wind.

I might wonder at their ability
to take flight, and leap, and
change direction in an instant.

I might think of them,
of all earth's creatures,
as my most kindred spirits.

In the Meantime

Long before I came to sit and look into the sky,
that bird made its way from tree to tree -
that I have built a house beneath its home
is cause for neither pain nor pleasure
to one who is always who it is.

Years from now, when all that fills my heart
has finally been emptied,
a bird will make its way from tree to tree.

In the meantime…

On Reading Rexroth's Japanese Poems

I
I look to the mountains in the east,
peaks shrouded in snow,
and wonder of the storms
which trouble them.

II
Sparrow on the wing
takes no thought of me.
I spend the night
dreaming of its flight.

III
The bamboo whispers against the night,
restless and uneasy in the breeze.
I lie in bed, listening,
pretending to sleep.

Nothing

Nothing is happening here.
Nothing is being earned.
Nothing is being produced.
Nothing is happening here.

Nothing will happen here.
Just the sea...
the wind...
the birds...
the otters…

The Bridge

Beneath this bridge
a river runs
swollen with storm rain and debris.
Trees toss barren branches
before the muddied procession.
A pale sliver of moon
reflects the rippling currents,
revealing my shadow shivering swiftly
in the night.

Spring Forward, Fall Back

We turn back time today
to reinvent what we tell
ourselves about ourselves.

We reset and synchronize,
taking the inventory of an hour
to remind ourselves of all
we do not know.

Spring Sun

The spring sun poured through
closed classroom windows, and spilled
on the floor in puddles of warm light.
Nearby, the trees trembled restlessly
with the songs of birds -
faint and filled with longing.
The breeze caressed a world
alive with desire and music and light.

The Illahee

The creek slipped through a crack
running along the hidden heart of the place,
life surging beneath a tree
anchoring in the earthen soul.

Through long years the creek
kept a secret from the salmon
bending by its narrow banks,
waters singing softly, sweetly below the breeze.

Listen long enough, the tree sighed,
and the secret could belong to all with
patient, peaceful interest in the mystery.

The creek still runs and sings,
the tree still sighs along the breeze
and the secret still waits.

II. head home together...

Runaway

From chaos you fled
to a world you could never love,
and which you knew
could never love you.

Where did you go, little boy?
What secrets did you hold in your heart?

I, too, run away to another world,
carrying my own secrets.
I will look for you there,
and if I find you,
we can head home together.

Water Bearer

A buzz cut boy with a garden hose
makes mud in the afternoon sun.
He waves the water as with a wand,
watching patterns in the air and earth.

He does not worry where water comes from,
knows nothing of where it goes.
Enough for him to see a puddle
and feel the dark goo in his hands.

He laughs at a river he creates
along the garden bank, and at
bits of twig and bark he sends
down the slow current.

Fifty years from now he will remember
and recognize his life - a bit of bark,
a slow swirl, hands full of mud -
and marvel at its mystery.

Rainy Day in the Little Woods

A quarter mile from home,
fallen branches arched against
a granite boulder and formed a lodge.

Beneath the smell of pine pitch,
random raindrops tapped our
coats, jeans, and boots in secret rhythms
we would not repeat to anyone.

Fifty years ago in that sacred space
we dreamed far from our lives
and spoke in many directions.

The wild winds danced
through the trees overhead,
danced until we were dizzy
with wonder and imagination.

Night Rain

I would smell the rain
before I heard it.
Through the open bedroom window
would come a thin, metallic scent
in the night, with hints and promises
thickening the air to audible liquid.

I could envision dark, dense grass
drinking in silence,
huddled evergreens shivering at a touch,
the roof complaining as pebbles worked free
from the tar, spiraling down the drainpipe
just outside, a foot from my pillow.

Nothing since has spoken so clearly,
or smelled as good.

Uta I

Dark mountain, blue dusk,
ferry waking the Sound.
Escorting gulls
keep on circling the ship
coming into Seattle.

Uta II

With the sun now gone
the waves are left to themselves
to find their way home.
How slowly they move to shore.
How softly they touch the sand.

In a Dark Dawn

In a dark dawn,
tires hiss up and down the Avenue.
Lights from shops not yet open
fall on my feet as they slip
toward the future.
I duck into a sandwich shop -
thirty years from now,
this morning will still be unwilling
to be forgotten, and I won't know why...

Weekend in Victoria

A little boy looks out a hotel window
at a harbor of boats and birds.

His eyes dart and dive
and seem to see everything.
He calls out the names he knows,
and what he cannot name
he tracks in silence before asking –
"Wassat?" Wassat? Wassat?"

One by one I give him
all the names I know
and all my guesses.
He judges nothing,
having only wonder with which
to trace the world.

How long has it been
since I saw the world that way?
How long will I need
to look into his eyes
before I see that way again?

Just North Of Clifden

Four in the morning there
as dark waves flash lights
on the boulders along the shore.

An abandoned processing plant,
the houses of those who don't live there,
and perhaps a ghost or two.

I knew the ancestors of those waves,
and of the birds who rode their backs,
crying endlessly through the late afternoon.

Even from far away
I can hear the end of the world.

Drawing From Memory

It is too early, far out
in the Dingle morning,
thousands of miles from here.

Clouds that will be gray at daybreak
drift darkly over the North Atlantic,
as rain raps the stone roofs
of ancient shepherd huts.

A small fire could still keep you warm
in those humble hives,
as might the memory
of those who spent nights there
down through long centuries.

From this warm room,
I remember and dream the night away.

The Trail Of Your Life

Anyone following the trail of your life
would believe you are lost.
You yourself have often wondered
at the bends and switchbacks,
the fallings and risings,
and have despaired of arriving anywhere.

And yet you keep on,
knowing you near the end -
even if the end is only the place
from which you will watch
the path extend beyond you.

Merry Go Round

We are told the world is spinning,
and as it spins, it also circles the sun.
No wonder we are so dizzy
we can never keep our feet.

We ride the merry-go-round.
Bracing ourselves in the center,
we are spun faster and faster
whirling through the playground.

We hold on until it slows and stops,
then stagger off like retching drunks.
Finally, we tumble to the ground,
grasping the earth beneath our backs.

III. impatience...

Impatience

I read the book of poems
from back to front,
unable and unwilling to wait.

Beginning at the end,
I read what was written before,
and am left at the start
of a journey I cannot make.

A Far Morning

You wake in your world
and I in mine,
in this time that belongs
to us, but not to us.

Having shared so much life,
we now have only hope
for a future we must invent
as it arrives, uncertain of return.

Everything we always thought was ours
turns out to be a dream
from which we fear to wake,
from which we must wake,
to discover who we are.

In Wonder Land

I have just thrown myself
completely through the sliding glass door.
I have done it when no one is at home,
in the middle of the day,
when everyone is at work.
I came home, patted the dog, took three steps,
and plowed through the closed door.

If Alice could go through glass
and find another world, so can I.
Having gone through the door,
I can now bleed my way there.

Looking Over My Shoulder

I seek the life
I never lived
as I walk in the dark morning.

I look for it in every person.
I listen for it in every song.
I pray for it in every sun.
I dream for it in every moon.

But I know
I left it far behind
in a place to which I can never return.

Tanning

She comes to the beach
and spreads her blanket on the sand.

Seen, and pretending not to see,
she unbuttons her blouse
and lets it fall.
Stepping from her sandals and skirt,
she anoints herself with oil
and prostrates in the heat of mid-summer.

Shimmering, head thrust back, eyes closed,
she receives the fullness of the sun.
An offering in a parody of love,
she lies on the beach.

Spinning In The Dizzy Dance

This story you are telling yourself
has come to an end, but you don't know it.
The true story is a mystery -
the occasion of your own life.
Are you able to hear what the story will be?
Are you able to see what you will become?

What the world will hear and see,
is unfolding before your eyes, but
behind your back.
And there you are - spinning in the dizzy dance -
trying to see your own blind spot.

The Big Bang

The universe explodes, and
constellations fly from me -
my brain blown to oblivion,
my heart flung like a star
across the night.

Is there no end to the ways
worlds find to fall apart?

IV. holding on...

Holding On

Reading in bed at night
it takes all my strength to keep living.

I remember the dead
in their coffin of winter,
and shiver – my sign of life.

I remember standing on a hillside
at the grave of my grandfather,
my toes touching the edge of his headstone.

I imagined his body in a box
deep in the frozen earth,
with only the grass to keep him warm.

I remember a friend kneeling
at a father's grave,
the knuckles of his left hand deep in the grass,
right hand holding his chin steady.

A light rain fell
as if heaven were weeping,
grieving the earth's dead
as they slept in their last beds.

Tonight I, too, weep, knowing
I must join them in sleep.

For Craig

A year or so later, we went on
without you, into the real world,
leaving you below in the real earth.
I've lived in many worlds since then,
knowing you've been dead for all the lives
I've lived in every one of them.

I imagine you from time to time,
rotting quietly in your resting place.
I imagine you at peace,
resting quietly in your rotting place.

As for me, I'm tired all the time and
I'm running out of worlds and lives.
I can't imagine sympathy from you,
who lived barely one, and that one stolen.

And I still can't do a thing about your death,
other than give you
these few moments of remembrance,
after which you will still be dead.

Gibberish

She is slowly breathing out
the last of her life.

Her chest rises and falls
as waves do before a storm.
Her eyes open now and then,
and they narrow as if trying
to make out my face in the dark room.

Her finger points at the wall.
She mumbles incoherently
as she grips my hand.

I pat and pray
the storm will pass quickly.

Morning Tea At Jitters

I drank tea
one table over
from the mother of a serial killer this morning.

No one knew…
The barrista didn't know.
The gay Asian didn't know.
The mother didn't know -
nor did her son, who would be born
four months later in the spring.

My knowledge was not power,
but powerlessness – an awareness of all
I can do nothing about.

Intensive Care

He is dead now,
and what remains
are condensations of her guilt.
She speaks sweetly,
patting his hands and face,
weeping apologies, offering explanations,
seeking forgiveness.

But he is cooling more quickly than tears,
turning to stone before her eyes.
There will be no mercy, no benediction -
only the idolatries of shame.

She will not be absolved
from the sins of carelessness.

The Last Testament

In the end, a man destroyed
the heavens and the earth.
He said, "Let there be light"
and there was light.
The earth was fire and melted -
without form and void.
And then darkness was upon the face of the deep.

No seas, no soil
no flower, no forest
no beast, no bird
no man, no woman
only the dead, and the dying,
and the deep, radiating darkness.

Blessed is the darkness,
for it overcame the light.
Blessed are the dying,
for theirs is the kingdom.
Blessed are the dead,
for they need not inherit the earth.

Night Terrors

In desolations of darkness,
thick with fear and terror,
the mind wanders lonely
in search of something
not named or felt,
but desired or hoped.

Where is the dream
that will awaken?
Where is the dawn
that will break the spell?
Where is the heart
that will dare to believe again?

Pre-Dawn

Awakened by unremembered dreams,
I lie sleepless in the shivering dark.
Watching clock digits dimly illuminate
    the morning,
I grieve the future passing of my wife
    and children,
and imagine the deep, cold darkness of a
    world without them.
How desolate will be the pre-dawn then,
even if my dreams should come to me.

V. a river that flows...

There Is A River That Flows

There is a river that flows
by the house of my childhood.
It began to run when I left
and has followed me everywhere since.

With effort against the current,
I can swim upstream anytime
and see things as they were –
or as I was.

See that tender, naïve woman?
My mother.
See that wounded, frightened man?
My father.

See how each in their way
tries to get everything right -
life, love, children…

I watch their confused, tortured care
and let myself float back to this day,
no longer fighting currents or memory.

Letting everything be what it was...
Letting everything become what it will be…

Friends Long Absent Are Coming Back To You
(from a fortune cookie)

Who are they, and
where are they coming from?
When will they be here, and
how will they come?

What have they been doing, and
why have they been gone so long?
What was our parting like, and
how will the returning be?

Friends, long absent,
are coming back - to me.

How I Like It

I prefer it spare,
like a desert at night,
with no light to make things clear.

I prefer the hint
the shadow, the echo,
something not quite seen in the corner of the eye.

Let me dream for myself,
and imagine in solitude
what the words do not say.

Let the cup spill,
and the liquid run,
until it finds a place to rest.

She Comes To Me

She comes to me
undressed, eager and shy.
I cover her nakedness
and am covered.

In time, out of time,
our passions rise in rhythm
until they cry out, exhausted,
and our breath whispers secrets.

Scales

Your fingers play
along my spine,
light and quick,
up and down,
rehearsing scales
as beautiful as music.

Rain

Our words are rain falling
through the air between us
as the clouding darkness descends.
In your eyes are tears
from the storms from within me.
In the wet sting of the wind,
I feel your fury against me.
We stand facing, unable to turn
from the chaos of the coming night,
aware that sometimes even fools
don't know to come out of the rain.

Whatever Came Next

There were not enough nights like this –
settled into a chair,
loved ones nearby, safe.

Leaning against the spaces between us,
holding us together like mortar,
regrets come faster than whatever came next.

The Weight

Within the rhythm of your breathing
you sing the last measure of my life
on a scale only angels use...

The form of your stretching body
traces the constellation which will
lead me home through any darkness...

In your eyes I see myself seen
with all the grace and wonder words
hope to find but never do...

Years from now, when I am gone,
and you need to feel the weight of your life,
songs and stars and sights
will fill your arms, little one.

Baby Girl

Five weeks in your new world
and I am already crying for you.

The delicate perfection
of your fingers and toes,
the yearning plea
of your searching mouth,
the wondering eyes
of your innocent mind.

I hold them all, baby girl,
with a love I trust to be stronger
than the evil of these ruins
in which your life will be lived.

Shadowed by fears I pray
grace will one day drive away,
I hope only to die in your peace.

Repairs

The fourteen carat links
on this bracelet are so small,
I can barely see them, even with glasses.
I feel, but cannot fix, the confusion
of fine knots that will render this favored piece
of jewelry useless to my daughter.
Now, she too knows, with some sadness,
there are things in this world
even love cannot untangle.

Gone Again

You are gone again
across this vast, dark continent
which radiates your heat
like the desert after sunset.

If this is war, you win.
So I send a surrender
through the night, to where,
presumably, you still wait.

Wishes

She wishes she didn't have to wonder -
about the boy, about his words,
about his hands, about love and forever.

She wishes she didn't have to ask
whether he would be the one
who would touch her with the truth.

One Day

One day, outside a room far from here,
you will remember...
a drop of sweat slowly shivering
the length of your spine...
or the sound of your voice making
the vow that will be your future...
or the feel of a hand that somehow
became yours in the holding...

And in that trinity of remembrance,
you will look back along
the corridor of your life,
and see us who loved you
still with you, though left behind...

Paradelle at 50

I have kissed goodbye forever all our youth.
I have kissed goodbye forever all our youth.
What remains is all the future we have.
What remains is all the future we have.
We have forever all our goodbye youth.
The kissed future remains what I have.

The children will never know.
The children will never know.
They will find their own way.
They will find their own way.
The way their children never find
they will own, will know.

How can we ever learn?
How can we ever learn?
We keep reinventing ourselves.
We keep reinventing ourselves.
Can we learn, reinventing
how we ever keep ourselves?

All we children have kissed goodbye,
our own youth forever find.
Their way is the future.
Never reinventing ourselves,
they will know what remains.
How can I ever learn?

Wedding Poem

All your roads led you here,
where under a canopy of clouds and stars,
waves sing hymns on the shore
from which you now sail.

At this still point in the spin of creation
are gathered all the hopes ever dreamed for you
before light ever dawned over the face of the deep.

Led by the Elusive Presence who holds us all,
you leave us who have held you
in our hands and in our hearts.

Leave us ...without a look back
              ...without a regret
              ...without a care.

Leave us ...and live.

Grandpa's Teeth

Grandpa's teeth were sunk
in a water glass on the bathroom sink.
They sat laughing, empty and grim,
at a joke they repeated to him
every morning until he died,
drunk and toothless.

Years in the Grave

Years in the grave,
my grandfather's ghost rises
to greet the morning.
There are no questions in his eyes
and all the tears
have been cried by others.

He says nothing to me,
offering no explanation or apology.
His cigarette has burned down
to his scarred fingers
and he looks thirsty.

"I walk in your footsteps, old man.
At times I feel you looking
at the world through my eyes."

He laughs a hoarse laugh,
walks out into the dawn,
and doesn't look back.

Zechariah and Gabriel
(from Luke 1)

He scared the hell out of me.
It's one thing to believe and another to see.
When it came to angels, I preferred to believe.

But he showed up one day at my work place,
interrupting my beautiful, dutiful routine - came
out of nowhere and stood by the altar, smiling.

Our conversation did not go well. I did not smile.
I was skeptical, suspicious and in the end
he decided it was better if I did not speak.

And so I was silent for nine months, except
for what I scribbled on clay tablets, like a child
learning an alphabet, or learning to add.

Eventually I returned to work,
always nervous at the altar after that,
never knowing what I might have to see,
or what I might have to believe.

Father and Son

Father and son are rarely easy together -
too much is missing.

One life where disappointments
have long overshadowed hope, and
another where expectations
cannot bear the weight of living.

Words are choked off, either unspoken
or else arcing short of their intention,
falling like stars into the darkness
while the moon watches.

Actions are rootless and furtive,
not daring to be open or real,
and all the gestures signal only
the weakness of flawed love.

Still, grace finds its way
through the cracks,
like heat coming home in summer.

Father Turns Seventy

In the middle of the winter,
in the year of the Depression,
you were borne into the world
by the dark heat of their desire.

Your parents, newly-wed, held you,
trembling in the knowledge
you had created them ,
with the joy that only terror knows.

Human, how could they raise their god?
Empty, how could they nurture their creator?
Flawed, how could they perfect their holy child?
Their love would not be enough.

But you, in your long mortality,
have won your costly freedom.

Who Knows What A Father Thinks?

Who knows what a father thinks?
Who holds the key to that door?

If I was a thief, I would break in
and enter his head -
during the day, when he was at work,
and I could take my time.

I would rummage through drawers,
look behind furniture, search under the bed,
tear off sheets and covers, if necessary,
looking everywhere for those hidden thoughts.
He wouldn't have a secret left
when I got through with him.

But... he's retired now,
and never leaves the house.
And the entrance to his head
is always, always well-guarded.

Words Not Spoken

In the end, my father
thrashed through the long nights of his dying,
both wanting and fearing sleep.

In a still, dark morning
he lay awake after dreaming, saying to my mother,
"Now I know what I need to say to Mike."

But no one ever heard those words - perhaps
they were eaten by what devoured his brain - or
maybe they were just a delirious declaration made
by a soul emptying itself before death.

In any case, they were with all that died with him.
Years later I wonder about those words.
Did he need to say them,
did I need to hear them... both?
Maybe they never really existed except in a dream.

I only know I still run my fingers along the scars
he left, for which no apology was ever given;
I tend the wounds which have never healed,
for which no witness was ever given.

There were not many words for me in his life,
and even fewer at his death. I am
surrounded by the ghosts of words not spoken.

The Face in the Mirror

Your life was a secret
I was never told.
With your death, the mystery -
already deep - deepened beyond wonder.

There are places in my life
where only you lived.
I still look for you there,
and am surprised to find you gone.

So much I want to remember,
so much I cannot forget,
so much I never knew.

I see your gifting and your wounding
in the misted mirror where I ought to be,
but I cannot see the part of me that was not you.

The ashes we scattered are proof of your passing,
no matter what the mirror reveals.

My life is finally my own.

Dream Father

It had been long enough.
I believed I would
no longer dream of you.
But last night there you were.

I was crying.
You came to me and asked why.
"You're dead. Life is short. The world
is a nightmare, and I can't protect the kids.
Take your pick."

You set your jaw as you always did
before you lost your temper.
But I ended the dream before you could speak.

Only a dream, I thought, as I awoke -
but my cheeks were wet.
At least I no longer have to hear
what you think.

VI. cannot unlearn the heart...

Love in a Red Field

Love in a red field
where no leaves have yet fallen.
The sun, by degrees,
makes slow arrangements
the eyes cannot follow.

All mysteries find
the same way home.
What the flowers know
will not be forgotten.
The foolish find they
cannot unlearn the heart.

First Mountains

Back before the town grew up
and the day was clear,
a small boy in his backyard
could face east and see the far mountains.

Too young to know what wonder was,
the boy simply stared at beauty
traveling the speed of light
to spend some time with him.

Later he would learn that the world
of his unknowing wonder, wondered back at him,
and would always be his friend.

Lover of God

(from Acts 1)

Fine. Tell me what you heard
from someone who was there,
though I doubt the truth
is told in such a story.

I am lover of God, whoever God is,
and a doubter of people, whoever they are.
I am tired of fables and tales,
and only a helpless hope keeps me listening.

All my life I've listened for God,
looked for God, dreamed of God -
only to hear you say it is for me
God listens, looks, and dreams.

So tell me the story,
and it had better be good.

Game Day Street Preacher

Suppose this old black man is God -
Jehovah in Salvation Army clothes...

Suppose this incognito deity,
marching the circle of the stadium,
is mediating grace through his madness...

Suppose the scoreboard clock,
counting down with each prophetic footfall,
marks the passing of the universe...

And suppose these cups of beer,
and fistfuls of bratwurst
lifted to ten thousand throats,
are the elements of a sacrament of despair...

Mornings Deep In Winter

There are mornings deep in winter,
when God wants company for a while,
and gently shakes your shoulder,
in a way that makes you think waking
was your idea.

You roll over,
hoping to return to sleep, but
you've thought too much to do it,
so wearily you rise, groping
your way through the pre-dawn dark,
with three more hours to kill -
if you have that sort of view of life,

In a while it may occur to you
that God might be up to something.
Sure enough, eventually, God emerges
from a favorite hiding place, and confesses
to the desire for your company.

So you begin the new day early -
but in the presence of a friend
who likes having you around.

Sent From God
(about John the Baptist)

What a strange journey
for mercy to make -
from a mother's womb,
down the birth canal,
into the arms of mid-wives.

He began to speak
along that dark path
into a baptism of light.

Later, he would search
the wild night skies
for what must come,
knowing another path
would be prepared.

He was not the light,
but spoke along the dark edge
so the world would know
what it was about to see.

The Revised Standard Version

Amid filmstrips and flannel boards,
I find the Bibles we cannot bear to throw away.
Presented long ago in solemn ceremony,
they yellow and decay as books do.
Old quotes and notes in pencil and pen occupy
the margins of pages unseen by any eyes for years.

I know these verses by heart,
by which I mean they live in my mind
and are as rhythmic as breathing.
But they, too, decay, discarded for other versions
which say what I want them to say.

Twenty years ago, these words answered questions
on which life hung.
They no longer seem true in those same ways,
but they are familiar and friendly.

I tell you the truth:
though these words will pass away,
we recite them again and again,
hoping to believe by repetition.

The Tribal Flute Player

I played for you as the sun rose;
dark, low notes from the river's edge
rising from the ground, walking
in rhythm with the flowing water.

I played for you when the sun was high -
notes that flew over clouds,
notes that dug into the earth,
notes that wound along the path.

I played for you as the moon emerged
reflecting the light of a dying day,
shining on the ground you walked
on the way to sleep and dreams.

I played for you in the night
from the depths of the sacred space
we call home.
Alone, I played the life we share.

Star Sonnet

The stars are silent tonight,
quiet fires aflame in space,
glowing dimly with shimmering light,
illuminating earth's ambient haze.

How pitiful the world must seem,
with all its mad idolatries,
to those who view its tortured dreams,
and watch its witless agonies.

And yet the stars which ring the moon
like pale mute choirs, stand
and, voiceless, witness doom
descending on the darkened land.

Still, revealing greater light,
the stars are silent in the night.

Sky Tree

I never wanted to be this high
and not know ground
or roots around rock.

One planted in the heavens
can never stand or stay
with trunk, branch, and leaf
made of vapor and cloud.

I tumble endlessly
in the dark, in the dawn,
vainly trying to hide
from the sun, the moon, the earth, God, you...

Love in a Blue Sky

Love in a blue sky -
beyond your reach...
holding your breath...
sheltering your world.

Where a bird's red wings
might trace the arc
of the sun's promise;
or a grasshopper
leap the length
of the moon's dream

The heart can believe
what the mind can't guess.
As hope heads for home
the heaven you have is enough.

Afterword

These poems were composed over a span of nearly thirty years and thus represent a wide variety of life stages and experiences. Some are clearly autobiographical, while others are purely imaginary, and still others combine both elements. I'll leave you to wonder about all that.

I want to thank: my mother, Patricia, whose love of poetry is directly responsible for my own; my fifth grade teacher, Marion Chadwick, whose assignment to memorize "Daffodils" by William Wordsworth stirred, and still stirs, my imagination; and my teacher and friend Wayne Connaway, who was the first person to call me a writer.

Made in the USA
Lexington, KY
10 January 2017